CU00802987

Basque Original Series No. 21

Etxe Roxenia

By Michelle Petitte

Center for Basque Studies
University of Nevada, Reno
2019

Etxe Roxenia
Basque Original Series 21

Center for Basque Studies
University of Nevada, Reno
1664 North Virginia St.
Reno NV 89577-2322 USA

http://basque.unr.edu

ISBN 978-1-949805-15-4.

Library of Congress Cataloging-in-Publication Data

Names: Petitte, Michelle, author.

Title: Etxe Roxenia / by Michelle Petitte.

Description: Reno, NV : Center for Basque Studies, University of
Nevada,

  Reno, [2019] | Series: Basque original series; no. 21

Identifiers: LCCN 2019025572 | ISBN 9781949805154 (paperback)

Subjects: LCSH: Bidegain, Arroxa Caminoa, 1864- | Women, Basque--
Biography.

  | Navarre (Spain)--Social life and customs--19th century.

Classification: LCC HQ1162 .P48 2019 | DDC 305.48/99920092 [B]-
-dc23

LC record available at https://lccn.loc.gov/2019025572

Contents

For Lina,

with love,

whose life and stories

embody

espiritu indarra,

strength of heart and spirit.

With special thanks to my sister
Kathleen Johnson
for creating
beautiful illustrations
for this story.

Ezbeharra, **The Accident**

Arroxa (Ar-osh-a) lugged a heavy basket of wet laundry up the bank from the washing stones by the river to the road above, half dragging it. Her arms ached from the work of scrubbing and rinsing. She paused part way up to catch her breath and brush her blond braid off her shoulder. It would be faster, she thought, to take the shorter but steeper path that ended by her *Aita*'s *errota*, grain mill. She lifted the basket and took a long step up. The loose dirt and stones scrambled under her foot. She felt herself tilting backwards and sliding. She fell, hard, skidding down, the basket tumbled, and clean clothes scattered. She felt her right leg slide out, her knee caught the edge of a jagged rock, the skin and muscle ripped. Pain shot through her body. She clutched her knee with scraped hands staring at the gaping wound. My leg, she thought, hysteria rising in her chest, my leg. She threw back her head and howled, "*Aita, Aita!*"

Pedro and his son Erramun were stacking heavy bags of ground corn in the *errota*, the mill, which was on the main road of the village of Bozate. They looked up when they heard Arroxa's frantic cries and ran. They hurried, sliding down the hill to her side.

"Roxa, little one," Pedro carefully straightened her bent, bleeding leg. She wailed grasping his arms. He grabbed a laundered wet shirt, wrapped it around the bloody knee, and gathered her in his arms.

Arroxa sobbed, arching her back. "It hurts, *Aita,* it hurts." The men carried her up the up the bank to *Etxe Caminoa,* the family home adjacent to the *errota.*

"Go get the doctor," he instructed Erramun, "and then Antonia." Pedro sat her in a chair, her leg propped up. Her knee throbbed, and she rocked with sobs. He dipped a cloth into a bucket of water and gingerly began to clean the wound of dirt and pebbles.

Erramun returned with Antonia. She hugged her sister, trying to hide her alarm at the sight of the gash. Then she helped her out of her blood-soaked dress and reassured her over and over, "The doctor is coming, it will be alright."

The doctor, an older man with graying hair and tired eyes, finally arrived. He lay his medical bag heavily on the floor. "Tsk, Tsk," he said examining the raw, red wound. "This is a bad cut." Leaning in, he pressed his index finger on the swelling around the knee, "There's fluid under her skin that needs to be removed to heal."

"Do what you must to help her," Pedro said, brushing Arroxa's blonde curls away from her red rimmed eyes.

They moved her to the kitchen table, leg stretched out on a sheet. Arroxa watched as he took a small sharp knife from his bag. "No, *Aita*, no," she shrieked, writhing up. Antonia and Pedro reached for her, holding her tightly in their arms.

"Keep her very still," the doctor said. Then with swift movements, he lanced the skin on either side of the knee joint. Arroxa gasped, screaming in pain. She clutched her *Aita*, eyes wide. The doctor poured water over the bleeding slashes, pressed down to stop the bleeding, then wrapped the knee in a length of muslin bandage. "Keep her still," he said. "Don't move the leg. In three days, I'll be back to check the swelling."

Pedro carried his sobbing daughter upstairs to the bed she shared with Antonia. He propped her leg on a pillow, foot angled out. He held her close, letting her cry, until she slept.

Etxekoak, **Those of the House**

The Basque enclave of Bozate, part of the village of Arizkun, lies in the Valle de Baztán at the southern foot of the Pyrenees mountains, in the Spanish province of Navarre. In the late 1880s, its three hundred inhabitants lived in a semi-circle of whitewashed two-and-three story homes with painted shutters and peaked red-tiled roofs. The church, with its red brick spire and bell tower, was at its center. Lush green pastures with grazing *ardiak*, sheep, surrounded the village, layers of round-topped mountains served as a backdrop.

Pedro and his wife Josephina were born in the village. They married young and raised eight children. He was the eldest son of the village *errotaria*, miller and had grown up in *Etxe Caminoa*, the family's two-story wood-frame home with a wide balcony under the eaves and sandstone blocks outlining the windows, doors, and corners. At his father's death, Pedro, the eldest son, inherited both *Etxe Caminoa* and the *errota*, as is the custom in Basque society. Together he and his wife and children worked the family *errota*.

The Caminoa family was well known in the village. Pedro was an honest businessman, respected for his fairness in measuring grain. He gladly assisted his *auzotarrak*, close neighbors, with the work of daily life, as was the Basque custom. Together they harvested maize crops, threshed wheat, cut fern, chopped firewood, slaughtered pigs. He had a ready smile beneath the *txapela*, beret, that crowned his head, a thoughtful demeanor and a kind word for all.

Josephina was generous in all ways, her blue-gray eyes sparkled, her laughter was warm and affectionate. She too was close to her *auzotarrak*, the women of her neighborhood, and ready to help when needed. She often took Arroxa with her to tend the sick, deliver bread to hungry families, assist the birth of babies, offer comforting words to those who mourned.

"We have been given many blessings, Roxa," she often said, "we must open our hearts to the needs of others."

The family attended village festivals and joined in the community work of mending bridges, sweeping streets, and maintaining the church and *pilota* courts. They were devout, faithfully attended Sunday mass, their children filled the family pew.

Arroxa, eleven, was their youngest child, with the blue eyes and fair curls of her mother. Their older children were grown and gone; Matxin, to a distant village to run his own *errota,* while Santiago and Bernardo to an even more distant Argentina to herd sheep. Graciana, was married and living in a neighboring village. Dominic, just eighteen, had joined the military. Antonia, fifteen, lived at home and worked nearby as a housekeeper and thirteen-year-old Erramun, helped his father in the mill.

* * * * * * * * * *

The previous winter, in 1875, influenza swept through Bozate, passing from person to person by coughs and sneezes. Within a week, nearly every home in the village had someone ill with chills, body aches, and high fevers. Death came within days, especially for the very young and the elderly. Houses of the infected were marked with white chalk on the door, the families quarantined inside. The village streets emptied of foot traffic. The church bells tolled daily to announce the dead.

The old doctor was quickly overwhelmed. Nuns went from house to house offering prayers and what medical aide they could. Josephina and other village women prepared pails of soup for stricken families and left them on doorsteps. As the numbers of deaths rose, a horse-drawn cart was driven through the village; the bodies wrapped in shrouds were placed on the cart and taken to the churchyard for burial.

When Josephina fell ill, Pedro cared for her himself in their bedroom near the kitchen. He refused to allow Antonia and Arroxa to enter the room. "Please, *Aita*," Antonia begged from the doorway, Arroxa at her side. "Let us help."

Pedro shook his head, "This is what your *Ama* wants. She worries that you will get sick. You must respect our wishes." The girls wept but did as their *Aita* asked.

Pedro held Josephina as she shook with chills and coughed blood. When she died, he wrapped her body in a linen shroud and carried her in his cart to the cemetery in the churchyard. He buried her in the family grave, beneath a round tombstone carved with a Basque cross. The priest, in his solemn vestments, alone attended, offering final rites and prayers.

The family home fell quiet and empty without Josephina's bustle of activity. Arroxa felt an endless, yawning loss in the bottom of her stomach. She walked from room to room, touched the chair where her *Ama* had sat, her side of the bed, the woolen shawl she had worn. How could she go on without her *Ama*'s smile, the comfort of her arms?

For Pedro, the only consolation was holding and soothing his youngest daughter. As he wiped her tears, he resolved to care for her as her *Ama* would have wanted.

When the illness in the village subsided, the family and their *auzotarrak*, walked together to the church, the sisters wearing black veils. In the Basque custom of offering light to guide the dead, they lit candles and prayed for their *Ama*. They placed small bouquets of flowers on the bare earth of her grave in the churchyard.

After *Ama*'s death and Antonia had returned to her job as a housekeeper, Arroxa took up the household tasks. She made the morning fire, prepared *talua,* corn cakes cooked on the grill, cleaned up, shopped and mended. She carried the basket of laundry and her *Ama*'s scrub board to the river to wash clothes. Her fall and injury devastated Pedro, consuming him with regret. "She shouldn't have been at the river alone to wash," he fumed to Antonia. "She's much too young." Antonia shook her head, sighing, "She's old enough to do this work, *Aita*, it was nothing but an accident."

Aldaketak, **Changes**

For three days, Arroxa lay in bed, her leg swollen, every movement painful. She cried until her face was puffy-eyed and mottled, her body warm and sticky. She drifted in and out of sleep, aware only of Antonia bathing her in cool water, *Aita* offering her sips of herb tea.

The doctor returned and removed the bandage. The gash was still gaping and raw, the wounds he had cut were bright red slashes, the leg was inflamed and warm to the touch. Arroxa could not bend her knee. She looked from her father to the doctor, eyes filled with fear. The old doctor shrugged, "It's not healing, there's contamination here. She could die, it'll be best to amputate."

Shocked, Arroxa clutched her leg sobbing, "No, *Aita*, no." Pedro, too, was stunned, then incensed. The thought of his daughter crippled, unable to walk, seemed impossible to consider. What kind of life could she have in a small village? Angrily he gathered her in his arms, "If she must die, she'll die with both legs."

Desperately, Pedro sought help. His son Dominic was part of an encampment of Basque soldiers in the valley below Bozate, near the village of Elizondo. It was 1875, Spain was in the midst of the Second Carlist War, a fight to determine who would be the next King of Spain. Young Basque nationalists, like Dominic, joined the army in support of the cause of Carlos VII, who had taken an oath in Gernika to support the

Basque Country's independence. Pedro knew a military surgeon attended the wounded in the camp, a man trained at the Spanish District Medical Academy. Surely, he would know what to do.

He put Arroxa on a bed of blankets in the back of a small wooden cart pulled by a mule and walked down the long road to the camp. She lay curled on her side, injured leg throbbing, a knot of fear in her stomach.

At Dominic's urging, the surgeon agreed to look at Arroxa's leg. He sat her on a narrow surgical table in the infirmary tent and, wordlessly, examined the wounds and cleansed them with warm water mixed with vinegar. Arroxa watched the doctor work. She felt her body loosen, soothed by his calm confidence.

"These wounds aren't healing," he said to Pedro. "There's danger of infection if they're not cared for."

From the table of medical supplies, he reached for a basket of chicken eggs. He broke one egg into a small bowl. Holding the shell in his palm, he used his fingers to peel the clear white membrane clinging to the inside. With one hand he gently pinched the wound closed and with the other, coated it with egg membrane. He held it a few moments until the membrane begin to congeal and form a thin, opaque casing over the wound. He repeated the same process for the two knife cuts. He wrapped the knee in strips of bandage.

When he finished, the doctor spoke to Arroxa's father, "The egg will protect the wound and help it heal. This will take time, so keep the area clean and wrapped. She should keep her leg still, no moving or bending the knee. Feed her bone broth for strength and, if she has fever, give her willow bark." He sighed. "Her wounds will heal, but the knee, that's another matter. The incisions are deep and destroyed the muscles and the knee has mended badly causing her foot to turn out. She'll walk, but with difficulty."

Tears slid down Arroxa's cheeks, she took a gulping breath of air.

"*Milesker*, thank you," choked Pedro. "You have saved my child."

* * * * * * * * * *

At home Arroxa slowly healed. Each day, before going to the *errota*, her *Aita* carried her to the balcony overlooking the village road and settled her gently on a sheep skin. Antonia brought her portions of bread, goat cheese, and broth before she set off to work.

From her perch, Arroxa watched the busy road: horse carts filled with hay and sacks of grain headed for market, housewives carried baskets with loaves of bread and earthen jars of milk from the shops, the village priest in his cassock strode purposefully to and from church. Her young friends stopped below the balcony to call greetings and share gossip. When the sun was low in the sky, their neighbor drove his herd of *ardiak*, sheep, down the street from pasture to their paddock, his black and white *txakur*, sheep dog, barking at their heels. He waved his *makila,* walking stick, in her direction. She watched for *Aita* and Erramun and Antonia. It was her favorite time of day.

The pain lessened. Arroxa felt her strength return and thoughts clear. Sitting alone one quiet afternoon, she lifted her hem to expose her leg, unwrapped the bandage, and ran her fingers over the scars left by the wounds. She moved her leg, lifting, stretching, turning her ankle. It felt stiff. The knee was scared and unbending, the calf thin and misshapen. Her left foot forced outward at an awkward angle. A knot of sorrow throbbed in her chest. She leaned over, stretched her body down along the length of the leg, and cried.

The neighboring women, her mother's *auzotarrak*, came to visit. They brought small treats, a pear or a bit of chocolate, and they gave her a basket of thread and needles and yarn. In the tradition of good neighbor, good friend, they taught her to knit and sew. Arroxa's fingers were agile and purposeful.

Arroxa began to move with effort around the house, pulling her injured leg along, stopping as a matter of course to lean on a chair back, table or door frame. She climbed the stairs, one step at a time. She helped Antonia with housekeeping, relearning how to bend and balance as she lifted and carried.

On her thirteenth birthday, Antonia gave Arroxa her first ankle-length skirt and shirt waist. She loosened her hair from its long braid and gathered the blond curls into a bun at the back of her head. Antonia covered it with a *zapi*, kerchief, knotted in place.

"You are a woman now," Antonia said. "See how pretty you are!" Standing before the mirror, her leg hidden in the folds of the skirt, she did feel grown-up and pretty.

Like other village girls her age, Arroxa could read and write, speak Basque and

Spanish, and her school days were finished. She had learned from her *Ama* and her sister all the skills of a housewife. She was old enough now to find work as a housekeeper, as her sisters had done. But this was not possible. So Arroxa, with Antonia's help, learned to cut patterns and sew seams, work she could accomplish seated. She earned money making and altering garments, sometimes adding detailed embroidery work, and soon earned a reputation as a reliable seamstress. In these ways, she made her contribution to the family.

On Sundays, she walked with her family to church, leaning on Aita's arm. She went with them to village festivals and to tournaments of *pilota*, Basque ball games. She sat at tables with the young people and watched them dance and flirt, fall in love and court. She went to their weddings and the baptisms of their babies. On Monday Market Day, she sat on a stool to sell vegetables and eggs. She watched the village life swirl around her: women carried baskets and gossiped together, men bargained with each other for the best price, young people gathered in groups, laughing and talking.

* * * * * * * * *

Antonia was offered a new position as a housekeeper for a wealthy family in Baiona (Bayonne), France. Arroxa shared in her excitement and helped her sew skirts and aprons and pack her few belongings for the journey by wagon to the coastal city. Arroxa envied her sister the opportunity to travel and to live in a bigger village. Even more, she mourned her company, her encouragement, her words of advice, their shared laughter.

Antonia sent letters to Arroxa describing her new life.

> *Baiona is such a beautiful city,*
> *streets with shops and cafés, buildings*
> *with many stories, and a river with*

> *delightful bridges to walk. Do you*
> *know there are shops selling only*
> *chocolates, the most delicious chocolate!*
> *On my day-off I can ride a train*
> *to Biarritz to see the ocean. How*
> *wonderful that will be!*

In a later letter, she wrote about a Jewish merchant she had met. His family owned a prosperous import shop. Within months, she wrote to say they were engaged to be married, and she invited Arroxa to visit,

> *He is handsome and so generous to*
> *me, Roxa. After we are married, we*
> *will live in his parent's beautiful house*
> *on Rue Maubec, and I will help in the*
> *family business. Come and visit us,*
> *perhaps for the wedding!*

When *Aita* heard news of the engagement, he became infuriated. A devout Catholic, he could not understand or accept his daughter marrying outside their faith. "Arroxa you're forbidden to go to your sister," he said in anger, "She's no longer faithful to our God and our church. Her marriage will never be blessed, and her children will not be baptized. She's no longer a part of our family."

Arroxa argued, "*Aita*, Antonia has a husband who loves her, she has a home. He can provide well for her children. How can this be so wrong?"

"I won't speak about this with you again, Arroxa. Pray for your sister, she'll surely need your prayers. But you're not to see her, this is how it has to be."

Arroxa was heartbroken. She saw nothing improper in the life Antonia had chosen. She'd never seen her father so angry and couldn't understand how he could turn his back on his daughter, dismissing her from their lives. Antonia was lucky, she thought, to have found this new life.

Arroxa wrote to tell Antonia of *Aita*'s anger. Antonia responded,

> *I am so sad, Roxa, to think Aita*
> *can't accept my husband and the life*
> *we are making together. Even more,*
> *I will miss you, little sister. It breaks*
> *my heart to think I have left you. I*
> *pray you will find happiness as I have.*
> *Please know you are always welcome*
> *in our home.*

In the years that followed, the sisters would continue to exchange letters and share news about their lives, but they never saw each other again.

Her brother Erramun was next to leave home. At eighteen he became engaged to the daughter of a fellow miller who lived in a nearby village. Soon after the wedding, the bride's father was offered a position at a larger *errota* across the border in a Basque village in France. Erramun and his bride decided to leave Bozate with her family, eager to share in their opportunity.

The Caminoa house was quiet now. At age fifteen, Arroxa was the only child remaining.

The days felt long, the rooms empty. She missed the comforting presence of her *Ama,* the companionship of Antonia, the noise and busyness of her brothers, all of the laughter and affection of a big family.

Bizilaguna Familia Da,
The Neighbor is Family

One Sunday as Pedro and Arroxa came up the church aisle after mass, the village priest drew them into the nave to speak with them privately. "You've heard," he said, "of the Bidegain family and their misfortune?"

Arroxa and her father knew the tragic story. The Bidegains were a young village couple with a son, Sebriano, and small daughter, Manuela. Walking home from church one day, the father slung his umbrella over his shoulder as he talked and laughed with neighbors. When he rounded a corner, an older gentleman, drunk on too much wine, stumbled against the father. The fall caused the tip of umbrella to poke into the older gentleman's eye, leaving the man partially blind. Angered at the loss of his livelihood, the man demanded restitution from the court. The local magistrate called Bidegain careless and sentenced him to two years in prison.

The prison sentence staggered the young family. Bidegain's wife struggled to feed and care for their young son and daughter. She relied on the church for shelter and on the charity of her *auzotarrak* for milk and bread. For Bidegain, prison conditions were wretched; cold and overcrowded. Prisoners were forced to labor and given little food or water. When Bidegain became ill, coughing and weak, no medical treatment was provided. Within months of his release, the father was dead. His wife also fell ill. Arroxa had joined with other village women to help care for the family. They brought small pails of soup, clothes and blankets. They tended the sick mother, made sure the children were dressed, fed, and sent to school, they kept the hearth warm and the room clean.

Pedro nodded, "*Bai*, yes, such a tragedy, Bidegain was wrongly treated by the courts."

"Be that as it may," said the priest. "Now the mother has also died. The charities of the Catholic church gave the family a room and parishioners have shared in providing food. We need a home, here in the village, for these orphaned children. I thought of you, Pedro. Perhaps you have room in your house? The church will assist you with their care. And when they are of age, we'll find them jobs." He glanced at Arroxa, "They could use the hand of a woman, as well."

Arroxa listened, a tight feeling in her chest. She thought about her own sense of loss when *Ama* died. She waited, head bowed, as *Aita* considered the priest's request.

Ama's words echoed in her head, "We must open our hearts." He was a generous man, Arroxa knew.

Finally, he spoke, "Perhaps this is God's will," he said, "He's given me many blessings, this we can do in return." Arroxa's heart gave a small leap. She would have these young children to care for, their company in the empty rooms of the house. It was surely God's will they were sent her way.

* * * * * * * * * *

Sebriano Bidegain was seven years old and Manuela four years old, when they arrived at *Etxe Caminoa*. They had few belongings: some worn clothes, little wooden shoes, their mother's beaded rosary, a *txapela*, beret their father had worn. The first night, Arroxa made them a bed together in an upstairs room, feeling they would want each other's company as they adjusted together to their new home.

Sebriano was a quiet, serious boy, slender and wiry, with dark, watchful eyes. He made himself useful, helping Arroxa with her work, saying, "Let me do that," or "I can help." Several days a week, he would assist the priest at church, running errands, sweeping and cleaning. During milling season, he spent long hours in the *errota*, hand-sifting the newly milled grain to remove bran. He was hired by the neighbor to muck his sheep hut, and eventually, as a chore boy to help during sheering and lambing. Watching the sheep herders, he began to learn the trade.

Manuela had a sweet temperament and ready smile. She attached herself to Arroxa, following her from room to room, then outside to hoe weeds and throw feed to the chickens. She asked questions and chattered. Arroxa welcomed her company, she enjoyed braiding her dark hair, sewing small calf-length dresses, reading books, teaching her prayers. As Manuela grew older, she taught her housekeeping and sewing skills, just as her own *Ama* had done.

In the evening they gathered together for a meal, sitting around the table in the warm kitchen. After eating, *Aita* would light his pipe, relaxing his elbows on the table, and say, "Tell me a story of your day, children."

Manuela's face lit up and she eagerly recounted the household events. "Pedro, today we planted pepper seeds and I watered them with the pitcher all by myself."

Sebriano, reluctant and moody, needed gentle prodding from *Aita*, but he too talked about his day. Arroxa relished these evenings, remembering her brothers and sisters sharing stories this same way.

The priest arranged for Sebriano to work as a sheep herder on a *baserri,* farm*,* when he was eleven years old. The farmer provided a hut with a dirt floor and, each Monday, gave him a loaf of bread to tuck under his arm. This loaf, along with milk and cheese from the *ardiak*, were his food for the week. When the bread became too hard to eat, he would soak it in water.

Being a sheep herder was hard work. Each morning he rose before dawn. He milked the sheep, holding the squirming ewes between his legs and squeezing the creamy liquid into a bucket. Then he and the *txakur* drove the flock to the valley pastures. All day he circled the meadow watching the *ardiak* graze on grass and shrubs. He kept an eye out for wolves or fox, took care of injuries or sickness. At the end of the day, he drove the *ardiak* back to the paddock in the village for another milking. He slept on the dirt floor. On Saturday evening, he would return to *Etxe Caminoa*, tired and hungry. Sunday was his only day to rest and attend church.

Arroxa, worried about him, "He's too young, *Aita*, to be alone so much," she said. *Aita* shrugged, "This is how he'll learn the work of the shepherd. He's like all the other poor boys, he'll be fine." But she knew the nights were cool and sometimes rainy, so she made him a cape of rough wool to wrap around himself when he slept. And she noted with pleasure, *Aita* gave him his first *makila*, walking stick, he could use to guide the *ardiak*.

When Manuela was ten years old, the church arranged for her to earn her keep working as a maid in the home of an aging doctor in Donostia (San Sebastian). So young, Arroxa thought, this is what it is to be poor. She sewed aprons and simple dresses for her, as she had done for Antonia. When the wagon came to collect Manuela, Arroxa held her at arm's length, "You look grown up, you know how to do this work. It'll be good, Manuela, but I'll miss you." She kissed her on each cheek and gave her a hard hug, keenly feeling the loss of yet another sister.

It would be many years before Arroxa would see Manuela again. But the move to Donostia proved fortunate for Manuela. When the old doctor died several years later, he left her a small sum of money and a piece of property. With this as a dowry, she was able to marry. Her husband, a skilled cabinet maker, opened a shop on Getaria Kalea (Calle Getaria), near Zaragoza Plaza, one of the most fashionable areas of Donostia.

Gizon bat bihurtzea,
Becoming a Man

On a cool spring evening the priest called at *Etxe Caminoa*. He accepted a chair by the fire, a tumbler of *ardoa*, wine, then lit his pipe and exchanged pleasantries with *Aita*.

"I've come to talk about your future, Sebriano. And also, with you, Pedro," he turned first to Sebriano. "You've had your fourteenth birthday, my blessings."

"*Milesker,*" Sebriano nodded, leaning in, listening respectfully.

"You're a grown man now and, just as a child grows up and leaves his parents' home, the church expects you to provide for yourself. The church charities helped you, along with Pedro, but now that'll change," he said. "Pedro, if Sebriano is still welcome in your home, he must pay his way in rent."

"Bai, I too am thinking of these things. He's old enough to work in the mountains this summer," *Aita* said. "And in the fall, he can find work on the *baserri*, the farms, during harvest. We'll make an agreement about the rent."

So, it was decided. In late May, Sebriano left for the summer. He climbed with his flock and *txakur* above the valley pastures, past the woods of oak and ash. The villages disappeared from view, up to high meadows of lush green grass, to the solitary life of the mountain sheep herder.

He rose early, silver morning mist clinging to the hillsides. He milked the bleating ewes, filling and refilling a birch wood bucket, pouring the milk into round cheese molds. These he stored in a cool hollow dug in the back of the stone hut. During long days he followed the herd as they grazed up and down the slopes, their mounds of white wool radiant against the deep blue of the sky. He carried bread and cheese in his knapsack.

At dusk he rounded up the *ardiak*, his *txakur* weaving in and out, nipping at their heels, they drove them back into the paddock for a second milking. Then he tended a small garden of beans, potatoes, and carrots, fished for trout in the stream, foraged for walnuts and mushrooms, gathered firewood for warmth and cooking. He prepared his evening meal in a pan over an open fire in the doorway of the stone hut, the western sky turning red and orange to gray. He slept in the single room on a mattress filled with fern leaves.

Many days would pass when Sebriano did not see another person. Every few weeks the owner of the *ardiak* would climb the mountain to check on Sebriano and his herd and to collect the rounds of cheese. He would bring a loaf of bread, a bit of pork, and a *txakoa*, a goat skin bag, of red wine. Sometimes Sebriano would meet with another shepherd and they would spend an evening together, corralling their *ardiak*, sharing a meal, playing the card game *mus* by firelight.

Sebriano returned to Bozate in early October. From the balcony, Arroxa watched him, slender in his dark trousers, his hair grown long under his *txapel* and curling around his face, his *makila* in hand, knapsack with his few belongings slung over his shoulder. He was quiet in those first days at home, more than usual, as though the mountain had claimed his voice.

In the winter months, Sebriano took what jobs he could find on the *baserri* surrounding

Bozate. In early spring he worked in the maize fields, shoveled dirt clods, dug furrows, raked piles of manure, then planted seeds, one kernel at a time. In the fall, he labored in the hay fields, cut the stalks and spread them to dry, raked them into piles and loaded the huge bundles onto farm wagons. He would return to *Etxe Caminoa* at night, exhausted, eating a meal with Arroxa and *Aita*. He sat with them near the fireplace sharing small stories of the day. Each night he would say, "*Milesker,*" before heading up to his bedroom.

At twenty-two, Sebriano was muscular, his skin bronzed from hard work in the fields. He had earned a reputation as a reliable worker and made many friends among the young villagers. He met them for *pilota* games at the village *fronton,* stone court, and for dances at festivals.

Arroxa sat with her *Aita* and other adults at long wooden tables set up in the village square near the *fronton*, sipping *ardoa* from a tumbler. She watched, smiling, as Sebriano, a red sash tied at the waist over his white linen shirt and woolen pants, joined the others in the skillful foot work, agile jumps and high kicks of the Basque dances. Her feet tapped in time with the drum and the music of the accordion and *txistu,* flute. But her heart cried out with longing to rise up, to turn and twirl, to move with grace and ease if only for the evening.

* * * * * * * * * *

One Sunday after church, Arroxa noticed Sebriano standing near Maren, the daughter of a village shop keeper, shyly speaking with her. Maren was a slender sixteen-year-old, a quiet girl with dark curls and a sweet smile. How well they look together, thought Arroxa.

After dinner one evening, Sebriano remained seated at the table, his hands folded, his face serious. *Aita* lit his pipe, the sweet scent of tobacco filling the air. He looked at Sebriano and waited. "Pedro," he said, "you know Maren, the shop keeper's daughter?" *Aita* nodded. "I want to court her."

Arroxa knew, as did Pedro, what was left unsaid. Sebriano, a young man with no family and no property, would not likely be welcomed as a suitor. Basque tradition called for both husband and wife to enter marriage with a dowry, property or goods, to give the couple a start. Families often met together to discuss and make agreements before allowing the courtship and marriage of their children.

There was a long moment of silence, *Aita* puffed on his pipe. Finally, he said, "We'll go to her father together. I'll speak as your family. We'll see what we can do."

Relief washed Sebriano's face, "*Milesker,* Pedro. I'm again and always in your debt."

"You're earning your own way, Sebriano, I'm proud of the man you have become. Let's see what happens," he replied.

The marriage arrangements were made, the banns were announced at church. For Maren's dowry, her father gifted the young couple with a small house of two rooms, on a property with a garden, near the edge of the village. From *Etxe Caminoa*, *Aita* lead a small cart holding a marriage bed and mattress to the dowry house. To this, Arroxa added baskets of linens decorated with blue embroidery, bottles of *ardoa* and cakes adorned with ribbons. Sebriano and Marin married in the parish church, the bells rang. They celebrated with family and friends, feasting and dancing in the square.

Maren embraced Arroxa as a sister-in-law. She sought out her company at village events, often linking arms to walk together. The couple came to *Etxe Caminoa* for Sunday dinner. "It's good to see you, *Aitatxi*, grandfather," she greeted *Aita* with affection and respect.

Arroxa noticed the lightness in Sebriano's step and a ready smile. She would ask "Are you well, Sebriano?" He would grin back, nodding, "We are well!"

Maren became pregnant in their first year of marriage, her belly rounding on her thin frame. Sebriano, quietly proud and protective, walked her to Monday Market and to church. She went into labor in the early hours of the morning, *auzotarrak* in attendance. Arroxa heard the stories later, the baby stillborn, the midwife unable to stop the bleeding, mother and child lost.

The funeral cortege wound through the village from the dowry house to the churchyard. The priest in white vestments led, Maren's brothers and cousins carried the black draped casket next, and Sebriano and her *Aita* followed, head bowed. The women, her *Ama*, sisters, and aunts, came last, heads covered in black veils, their voices raised in prayer. Mourners threw handfuls of dirt on the coffin and offered lit candles. Arroxa wept.

The next time she saw Sebriano, he appeared stunned. She greeted him with concern, but he seemed unable to meet her eyes or to answer. "Give him time," *Aita* said, "it's hard, but he's strong, he'll survive." Arroxa prayed this would be true.

Etxeko-andrea,
Mistress of the House

Arroxa woke early in her upstairs bedroom in *Etxe Caminoa*. Soon she would get up and dress and make her way down the stairs to the kitchen to prepare *Aita*'s breakfast of coffee with warm milk and bread. But for a moment she lay and stretched her legs beneath the covers, allowed herself time to think and remember. She was almost thirty years old now, how was it possible so much time had passed? Her mind drifted back to her younger self, a lighthearted girl, feet nimble in rope sandals, heart filled with dreams of love and children and her own home.

Her leg, her injured leg, had changed everything. The long recovery, the many hours alone, had made her more pensive, more sensitive to the hardships of life. She was able to walk, but her movements felt cumbersome, graceless. And, although she had many friends her age in the village, no man came to court her. Her heart ached at the unfairness.

And her future, what was ahead for her? She knew, as an unmarried woman, she would always have a home in *Etxe Caminoa*. In Basque inheritance tradition, the *etxea* is sacred, it is said, "*The family belongs to the house, not the house to the family.*" When a parent dies, the *etxea* is passed to a son or daughter who will live there and care for it. Her *Aita* was the inheritor and man of the house. She knew someday he would choose one of his children to inherit from him and they would become the master and mistress. She would stay on, assisting the family with housekeeping and child care. Only for now was she the mistress of her father's *etxea*. Reluctantly, she was coming to accept this.

Arroxa was determined to make her life purposeful: she swept and scrubbed, planted and weeded, sewed and embroidered, fed pigs and collected eggs, sat on a wooden box at the edge of the river to wash clothes, one leg bent, the injured one straight. She helped the church with small charities and was available to help her *auzotarrak* with the chores of daily life, just as her *Ama* had done. She took produce to Monday Market. Her friends were married now, with small children underfoot.

In the evenings when *Aita* came home, she would ask "Are you tired? Can I bring you tea or *ardoa*?"

"Roxa," he would sigh, "you are a blessing to me!" They ate their meal together in companionable quiet.

One evening as they finished, Pedro reached across the table and took Arroxa's hand, his face serious.

"*Bai, Aita*. Do you have something on your mind?" she asked.

Pedro took his time to reply. "I spoke with Sebriano today about working in the *errota*," he said. "I am getting older and with your brothers gone, I can use the help. He needs the work and is willing to learn the trade."

Arroxa nodded in agreement, "He'll do a good job and you can use the help."

"He's a good man, Roxa," Pedro said. "He works hard in the fields and comes home alone every night to his house. It's been two years, now." He shook his head sadly. "It is not good for him to be alone; he needs a wife. I talked to him about you, and he's agreed to marry you."

Arroxa was stunned, "But *Aita*," she said shaking her head, "you've never said anything about this before. Why now, *Aita*, why?"

"Ah, Roxa, my child," Pedro noting her distress. He squeezed her hand. "I'm growing older and you need a home, a place to be when I'm gone. Sebriano will provide for you. In exchange, he'll work in the *errota* with me and learn the trade."

"I don't know, *Aita*," Arroxa said, tears stinging her eyes. "How can I marry him? He's like a brother! And what about you, you'll be alone!"

"You need to think and pray," he answered. "You'll see this is what's best. You'll have a home and I'll have peace of mind. Someday your older brother will come back to work the *errota* and live in the *etxea*. This is how it should be."

A marriage arranged by her *Aita*? This was not uncommon in Basque villages. But Sebriano? As a younger brother, he'd always been kind to Arroxa, offering to help if needed. But, her husband? This quiet, moody younger man? It was hard to imagine; she didn't know what to think.

Arroxa bowed her head. 'This is how it should be, this is what's best' echoed in her mind. And she knew with both trepidation and certainty, it would happen.

* * * * * * * * *

On a cool October afternoon in 1894, she dressed for the last time in her *Aita's* house. She wore a dark green skirt and new vest she had embroidered with small red and yellow flowers, her blonde curls bound into a white *zap*i tied in a knot at the nape of her neck.

"You're lovely, my Roxa," Pedro said enfolding her hand in his. And for the for the first time in so very long, she felt pretty. Arroxa took her *Aita's* arm and walked with him down the street to the old stone church. At the doorway they paused a moment, she leaned her head against his familiar shoulder, then they climbed the steps into the church.

Sebriano stood waiting in the vestibule. He wore his black wedding suit, his *txapel* in hand. Arroxa looked up to meet his dark eyes and, in a wash of emotion, saw only kindness and affection. He smiled and reached out, tucked her arm in his, and guided her up the aisle to where the priest stood before the altar.

The church bells rang. After the benediction, Arroxa, *Aita* and Sebriano led a wedding procession to Etxe Camiona. A long table was placed in the hallway and covered with *Ama*'s embroidered red cloth. The guests spilled out into the back garden. Arroxa and Sebriano sat in chairs, side-by-side, receiving good wishes and the plates and bottles guests brought to share: lamb stew with tomatoes and sweet peppers, white beans cooked with pork and onion, salted cod and potatoes, *ardoa* and fermented cider and a small Gateau Basque, cake of buttery pastry filled with almond cream. Music filled the air, *txistu* pipe and accordion, deep male voices sang traditional Basque songs. At the end of the evening, the guests surrounded Arroxa and Sebriano, his arm at her waist for support, walked them to the door of the dowry house, and bid them good night.

When she woke the first morning in the dowry house, Arroxa felt she was truly seeing it for the first time. The bedroom window had a seat overlooking the street, the kitchen a low hearth with cooking pots suspended over the open fire, the back door opened to a garden with a bench, and leeks, carrots, and beets growing in rows. It's mine now, she thought, silently acknowledging Maren's spirit. She smoothed the new bed linens into place, arranged her few dishes and cooking pots on the kitchen shelves, filled her mother's vase with wild flowers and placed it on the small table set for two.

To give the couple a start in their new life as husband and wife, *Aita* gave them a dowry gift of two pigs; one to fatten for food, one to sell. Sebriano thanked Pedro. "You have what you need," he replied simply.

The stout white pigs, tails curled, wandered the streets during the day, as was the custom in Basque villages, foraging grass, nuts and roots. In late afternoon, they herded them into the fenced pigsty Sebriano built near his chicken coop. In the early winter, they would join their *auzotarrak* for the annual slaughter of pigs. Neighbors helped each other to slaughter, butcher, and cure the pig with salt. The pork would hang in a cool attic to be used in soup and stews throughout the year.

As he promised, Pedro taught Sebriano the trade of the *errotaria*. In early autumn, they worked the fields with their *auzotarrak* harvesting the maize. It was shucked and bagged on the *baserri*, then brought by wagon to the *errota*. The two men worked long hours together in the dust and noise of the *errota*. Sebriano dumped heavy bags of grain into the hopper, kept a careful eye on the thick granite mill stones, listened to the steady pound and thump of the gears as they crushed the grain. He hauled the bags

of milled corn meal and flour up wooden
ladders to the loft for storage. Pedro paid
him in *lakas*, measurements of ground corn.
They used these to barter at the market for
coffee, sugar and salt.

In the off seasons, Sebriano again found
work on the *baserri*. In the winter he harvested
nuts and fruit or helped with the slaughter of
pigs. In spring, he sheared sheep, milked and
made cheese. He labored in fields to plough
and plant maize. In summer, he no longer
went to the mountains. He hired out to cut
fire wood or mend fences. He helped with
the hay harvest. For payment, he accepted
money or shares of food, to eat or barter.

Their shared childhood made it easy to
slip into the domestic companionship of a
married couple. Arroxa managed the small
house, prepared meals for her husband tended
garden, and cared for the animals. On Sunday,
she walked on his arm to church. In the first
week of their marriage, Sebriano made a small
wooden three-legged stool where she could

rest her stiff leg comfortably as she sat. In the evenings they pulled chairs side-by-side before the fire. As *Aita* had done, she asked Sebriano about his day, encouraged him to share his thoughts and feelings. The serious, watchful boy had become a quiet, considerate man. At Monday Market, she now sat among the village wives to sell her eggs.

Nire Seme-alabak,
My Children

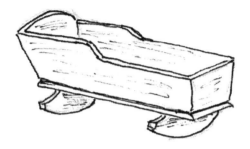

In the second year of their marriage, Arroxa found herself pregnant. It seemed like a miracle. She had thought, at age thirty-two, she was surely too old. She did not complain once of tiredness or her aching back, thinking only of the wonder of this child growing within her womb. Sebriano, too, rejoiced, stepping in to help her with chores, often admonishing her to sit and rest.

Arroxa woke on a cold November night feeling the sharp pains of labor. Sebriano immediately went to their *auzotarrak* for help and they brought the midwife. Then he paced as he waited, beside himself with worry. In the warm kitchen of the dowry house, aided by the women, Arroxa gave birth to a healthy girl.

Arroxa held the baby in her arms reveling in her little waving arms and kicking legs. "*Ongi etorri*, welcome, "she whispered, "I am your *Ama.*" She felt her heart would burst with love.

"I want to name her Saturnina after the Catholic patron saint of her birthday, Saturnin of Toulouse," Arroxa said, "this will bring blessings to her life."

"Saturnina, it's a good name," Sebriano smiled, gazing at the beautiful, dark haired girl, "but she's too small for such a big name. She'll be little Lina."

"Lina," Arroxa responded smiling, "*Nire txikia*, my little one."

Lina was a bright, happy baby. Arroxa swaddled her in cotton cloth and carried her in a soft sling close to her heart as she went about the day. Sebriano made her a simple wooden cradle and placed it near their bedside. Each night they rocked her to sleep, offering prayers to God for the blessing of this child.

Her birth was celebrated by family, friends and *auzotarrak*. They sent small gifts of sweets, *ardoa*, knitted blankets, and caps. She was baptized in the arms of her *Aitatxi* Pedro at the font in the nave of the church, blessed by the priest.

She grew and soon toddled around the dowry house in small rope sandals and dresses Arroxa embroidered with tiny Basque sunflowers. They marveled at her lilting voice, dark eyes, winsome gap-tooth smile, and her endless curiosity. Arroxa watched with pleasure as Lina ran to the door each evening to greet her *Aita*. Sebriano lifted her in his arms, laughing as she encircled his neck with a hug. Watching them, Arroxa understood better the love of her own *Aita*.

When Lina was a year old, Arroxa, to her delight, found herself pregnant again. Antonio was born on a warm July afternoon. He was named after her sister, Antonia. Different from Lina, Antonio was quieter, observing the world with a serious little face.

"He is just like you, Sebriano," Arroxa laughed, "see how he watches everything!"

Lina adored her little brother, calling him Tony. She rocked his cradle to comfort him, dangled flowers and feathers in his face to amuse him. Arroxa and Sebriano were content with this life together, these two beautiful children seemed to fill the dowry house with love and light.

Arroxa's brother Dominic had returned to Bozate. Married now, he, his wife, and teenaged children lived in *Etxe Caminoa* with Pedro and he had taken over the general running of the *errota*. Pedro, gray hair beneath his *txapel*, retired from the hard, day-to-day work of the *errota*. He had time for card games of *mus* in the village café with other old men. He often visited Arroxa, happy to sit in the little garden behind the dowry house, smoking his pipe, watching his grandchildren play. He would bring sausage and ham to share with the family.

Pilar, curly haired and beautiful, was born in their fifth year of marriage. Arroxa's heart was full and her days busy. Lina, almost three years old, was a confident child with a big imagination. She amused herself with simple toys, including a small doll Arroxa had fashioned of fabric scraps. Antonio at thirteen months was full of energy. He had learned to pull himself to his feet and toddle across the room.

The little dowry house seemed to have grown smaller. The bedroom now held their marriage bed, a baby cradle, and a stuffed pallet for Lina and Antonio. She did her best to stretch the harvest of their garden and eggs and meat from the animals. She made soups of beans or cabbage, corn porridge, and egg custard to feed their little appetites. She no longer had the time to earn money sewing for others. Now, she made baby shirts and diapers, she knitted small caps and socks and blankets.

Arroxa missed her mother in ways she had not imagined, longing for her advice and assistance. In moments of exhaustion, she would recall her patience and affection, her reminders of the blessings God had given. She was grateful for her *auzotarrak*, her own friends and her mother's friends, who offered help and companionship, as was the Basque custom.

With the new responsibilities of his family weighing on him, Sebriano continued to look for work in Bozate and on nearby *baserri* in the off-season from the mill. When he was paid in wages, often sixty cents a day, the money was quickly spent on food, sugar and coffee, wheat flour and cheese. He fished for trout, gathered firewood, scythed ferns for animal bedding, hunted for mushrooms, bartering these services for supplies. In exchange, farmers gave him goat milk for the children, honey and fruit, wool to knit into clothing.

At night, while the children slept on pallets in the bedroom, the husband and wife sat before the hearth fire in the dowry house talking and worrying together about how to make ends meet. When Arroxa found herself pregnant with a fourth child, she sighed deeply, "How will we manage?"

Sebriano sat in silence a moment, looking at the fire, "I could travel to Elizondo. It is a bigger village, maybe there will be work for me to do," he said.

The thought alarmed Arroxa. How would she cope alone with the children and the house while he worked far from home, even for a short time? How would Sebriano fare without the family to return to each night?

But they had to do something, that was clear. "Maybe it would be best to try," she said.

Another answer came days later. Pedro arrived one evening with a letter from Arroxa's brother, Erramun. He was the miller now in the small village of Urepele, just across the border in France. He had been offered a position at a mill in a larger town and was moving with his family. He asked if Sebriano wanted to be the new *errotaria* in Urepele. The position was his to take.

Sebriano and Arroxa listened without speaking, considering this offer. "This is an opportunity," Pedro urged Sebriano, "you're ready to be *errotaria*, you've learned well and know the trade."

Arroxa spoke first, "*Aita*, how far away is Urepele?"

"Just over the mountains," Pedro said, "You can reach it in one day by mule, you won't be far. It's a small village, but in the Vallée des Aldudes, where there are many *baserri*. They hire workers, Sebriano, which is also an opportunity. And Roxa, your *Ama*'s cousin, Josepha lives in the village. Her family owns a house near the *errota*, they'll offer reasonable rent."

Arroxa met Sebriano's eyes, she nodded. "We have the house here, perhaps we can find a tenant," he considered, "with the money we can pay for the mules."

"*Bai*, and I'll help you," Pedro said. "It's a chance you can't pass up. It'll be a relief to know you are settled and have work. And, also, a sorrow. But you won't be far, and that's a comfort."

So, it was decided. They would exchange their house and property in Bozate for a house and *errota* in the French village of Urepele, for an opportunity of steady work. Arroxa would leave behind the home of her marriage and the village of her childhood. And her *Aita*.

Euskalherriko Arkua,
The Basque Country Arc

Arroxa's leg ached and ached. She longed to
sit, even for a moment, to prop it on the stool,
to feel the pain ease, to close her eyes, to be
still. She shuffled-around the stone floor of
the kitchen leaning heavily on her strong leg.
The new baby, swaddled in sheep skin and
wrapped in a cloth sling, hung at her shoulder,
asleep. He had been born in late September.
Arroxa christened him Caminoa, her family's

name, but Sebriano called him Manuel, a middle name given the baby in honor of his sister Manuela. Manuel was a tranquil baby, eager to nurse, easily comforted. His birth had come at the end of milling season in Bozate. Sebriano had helped with the heavy work and now, October, the time had come for the family to move.

Through the open front door, Arroxa could see four-year-old Lina and three-year-old Antonio squatting on the ground occupying themselves rolling marbles made of river clay into a small wooden cup. Lina chattered as she played, directing the action, "No, Tony, like this!" and "My turn!" Her head tilted sideway, dark braid falling over her shoulder, as she aimed and nudged the marbles. Antonio watched and did his best to imitate. One-year-old Pilar, her hair a curly tangle, sat on the doorstep sucking her thumb and clutching her small scrap of blanket, sleepily watching.

Today was packing day. Sebriano had hired a local mule packer, Francisco, to transport the family over the mountains. Francisco knew the route well, he made many trips delivering goods and people over the border. He traded regularly with the family who owned the small store in Urepele and could take them to their new home. Francisco was, in addition, a *contrebandier*, a smuggler, who supplemented his income by carrying Spanish wine and other goods, across the border to the markets in France. Smuggled wine was duty-free, less expensive, and a very profitable business; he would dress in dark clothing, load his backpack or his mules with *txakoa*, sheepskin bags, filled with wine, sherry, and port, and traverse the many forest paths through the woods known only to Basque sheepherders. This morning he had arrived early bringing four woven baskets for Arroxa to pack. Tomorrow the family would make the day-long walk up and over the arch of Pyrenees Mountains.

The evening before, their *auzotarrak* had gathered in the yard of the dowry house to wish them goodbye. They brought small plates of food to share; thin sliced ham, potatoes sautéed in parsley, fresh goat cheese. They raised glasses of *ardoa,* toasting Arroxa and Sebriano's move, wishing them well. Arroxa watched their familiar faces as they laughed and talked, memorizing the warmth of their friendship.

Now, so much to do! Surrounding her, on the floor and table, was the stuff of her meager household, a cast iron pot and a water pail, wooden dishes, utensils, a kettle, wool blankets and bedding, lamps and tallow candles, a pile of clothing. She picked up items to wrap and fold. The saddle baskets, along with an assortment of bundles and wooden boxes, were all the two hired mules could carry. For Arroxa, the hardest part of packing was deciding what she must learn to live without.

Arroxa had written to her cousin Josepha Caminoa about renting the house. Josepha had married into the Marticorena family and lived in their home. She had written to tell Arroxa about the small house built by the Marticorenas across the road from the mill and very near her own home. Josepha wrote,

> *It is in need of repairs as it was damaged by a fire, but I think, with some work, it'll do well for your family, and you will be so close by! I look forward to having my cousin as an auzotarra!*

They would leave in the morning, Arroxa felt a knot tighten in her stomach. She knew the dowry house had become too small for her growing family; she knew Sebriano was pleased with his new position as *errotaria*. But in her heart, Bozate was home, her *Aita* was here, her friends were here, her memories, too.

A commotion at the door caught her attention. Lina cried, "*Aitatxi*, grandfather, *aitatxi*!" Her *Aita* appeared, laughing, stooping to receive Lina's enthusiastic hug, "We have marbles, *Aitatxi*!" she exclaimed.

"I see you have a game," he said, gathering Pilar in his arms and coming in the doorway.

"*Aita*," Arroxa stepped into his warm embrace, and rested her fair head on his chest.

"You're leaving early," he said, "so I came today to see my grandchildren, and wish you well on your travels, Arroxa. And I brought chorizo and apples for the road tomorrow." He handed her a bundle.

He looked down at her face, met her blue eyes, stroked her cheek, "No tears, Roxa. We're not saying goodbye. I'm your *Aita* and Bozate is never far away. I'll see you, all of you, at festivals." Arroxa took a deep breath and blinked back her tears.

* * * * * * * * *

They rose early. In the silvery dawn light, Francisco and Sebriano loaded the mules with baskets and boxes and bundles, covered them with canvas tarps secured with knotted rope. Arroxa prepared breakfast, dressed the children, then, for a final time, swept the floor of the dowry house with a straw broom, closed and latched the door.

Francisco led the first mule. Pilar and Antonio sat perched atop the saddle baskets, their little faces just visible. Sebriano led the second mule, in his wooden shoes, *makila*, in hand. The mule carried Arroxa with Manuel in his sling, bundles draped and tied all around them. Lina, in her rope sandals, walked beside her *Aita,* small footsteps beside his bigger steps. The passage over the mountains with heavily burdened mules and small children would take most of the day.

Lina had pouted tearfully when first told there was no room for her on the mules, "It's not fair, *Aita*, I want a mule ride, too."

Sebriano noted the hurt in her brown eyes. "But you're a big girl!" he said, "Who else will walk with me? Who'll help me guide the mules and keep track of my *txakur*? This is an important job!"

So, Lina walked, arms pumping, strong legs carrying her up the path, *txakur* trotting nearby. Sebriano encouraged her, held her hand and offered an occasional piggy-back ride. "Look at me, Antonio," she bragged from her roost on his back. "*Aita*'s giving me a ride!"

Early morning clouds shrouded the mountains, their solemn blanket of gray echoed the ache wrapped around Arroxa's heart. The tile roof tops and stone church spire of Bozate grew small then receded from view. The caravan plodded up the southern face, through woods of beech and ash, past shrubs and clusters of rock. They crossed the high grass meadows where sheep grazed in the summer, past the shepherd huts of piled stone.

"I have to pee, *Aita*" Lina said during the long, slow uphill. Sebriano walked her to the side of the road, held up her skirt as she squatted.

"Here, *txikia*," he pulled his handkerchief from his pocket for her to wipe. Lina's eyes lit up, *Aita*'s handkerchief! A gap-toothed smile of delight filled her face.

They paused at noon to rest and eat. Arroxa, cramped from the long ride, was eager to stand and stretch. She lay Manuel, tiny legs kicking, on a blanket in the grass. They ate a meal of *talua*, chorizo, apples and sipped *ardoa* from a *txakoa*, sheepskin bag. Antonio and Pilar chased after Lina, scrambling up the grassy slope of the trail, and rolling down. They filled their pockets with round stones and tiny flower bouquets.

In early afternoon, they crested the mountain, crossing from Spain into France at a border marked only by a lone stone post bearing the number 146. The path narrowed, skirting the hill, angling steeply downward into the Vallée des Aldudes. Before them spread a panoramic view. The hills, green and creased, hugged the edges of the valley floor. The River Nive wound through the valley, a tree-lined snake. Verdant meadows sloped back upwards to meet the line of woods, birch, pines, and chestnuts, their leaves tinged with autumnal oranges and yellows.

"Look," Sebriano said, leaning down and pointing. In the distance they could catch a first glimpse of tile roofs and a slate church spire, "That's Urepele, Lina, where we're going, your beautiful new home. It's not much farther now."

"This is beautiful," thought Arroxa, even as her heart ached.

The sky began to cloud and darken, the sun dipped from view. A cool wind came up stirring the nearby birch branches and ruffling the cloth covers on the loaded mules. Arroxa shivered and drew her shawl closer, tipping the sheep skin up to protect Manuel's face. She watched Pilar in the basket on the mule ahead stir from her nap, little fingers clutched the basket side, her gaze searched until she found her mother.

"*Ama*," she called. Arroxa smiled reassuringly, "Yes, txikia, I'm here. Look, we're almost there." Antonio sat, stoic, eyes taking in the distant view, his body swaying with the mule steps.

"I'm tired, *Aita*," Lina said. She stopped on the path, squatted with arms around her knees, and refused to move. Sebriano leaned down, scooped her up and settled her on his shoulders. She leaned in, head on his *txapel*, beret. "Rest a moment, *txikia*," he said. Her eyes closed.

They wound downward, plodding past thick groves of beech and pines. On the steep meadows, red Pyrenean cows and herds of wooly *ardiak* grazed. Scattered, *baserri* perched on the hillsides, the accompanying barns and vegetable gardens clinging tenaciously nearby.

On the valley floor, they followed the path, crossing the Nive over a crude wooden bridge. Sebriano lifted Lina up to watch the water churning and splashing. They turned southeast along the main road, following the river, and entered Urepele in late afternoon. The cluster of whitewashed *etxeak* crowded close to the road, green and red shutters closed to the ending day and cooling weather.

The mules trudged into the village square, past the *pilota fronton* and shops. At the general store, the shopkeeper's wife came to the doorway and called out, "Good evening, Francisco!" Then to Sebriano, "You must be the new *errotaria*. *Ongi etorri*, welcome to Urepele!" Sebriano raised his *makila*, nodding her direction. Arroxa smiled at the warm greeting.

Francisco guided the mules toward the church, a whitewashed building with a tall spire sitting on the crest of a hill. Then they turned right on a street between houses. He came to a stop in front of the *errota*, a brown stone structure with an arched doorway and high windows. One long wall was built down into the Nive. Arched openings allowed river water to flow in and out, powering the mill wheel. "That is the *errota*," he said.

"And that's the *etxea*," he said pointing. The house sat on the opposite bank of the river, just over a narrow bridge. It was a slender two-story structure, green shutters covering the windows, its whitewash worn away in patches. A side yard held empty chicken and rabbit coops; in the back an outhouse was built over the flowing river.

As Sebriano reached to lift Arroxa down from the mule, the doors of the nearby houses opened. Men in *txapelak*, berets, women clutching shawls against the cooling evening, came out, children followed, staring in curiosity.

"*Ongi etorri*, do you need help?" the neighbors said. Lina clung to her *Aita*'s leg, suddenly shy. In their baskets, Antonio and Pilar sat silent and wide eyed.

From the large house on the corner, Josepha appeared and hurried toward Arroxa, "You're here, finally," she said. "*Ongi etorri*, it's good to see you!" welcoming her with cheek kisses and a warm hug.

A commotion of greeting followed: Sebriano shaking hands, Arroxa trying to smile and focus, so many new faces. Manuel stirred in her arms and began to cry. Hands lifted the children from the baskets. Francisco began to loosen mule straps and unload boxes, baskets and bundles. Everyone helped carry them into the house.

Finally, Josepha waved the neighbors off saying, "We'll have time to visit, they are here to stay. Come Arroxa, let's go inside." She placed her arm around Arroxa and helped her walk down the narrow path leading to the front door.

Etxe Berria,
New Home

The house was musty, damp, and chilled. Pale
light came in the cloudy window glass. The
outside door opened to a narrow hallway.
On the right Arroxa saw a kitchen area with
a hearth and table and chairs. Behind it were
two smaller rooms. She climbed the narrow
stairs in the hallway. From the landing she
saw two bedrooms, one in the back and one
in the front, each with a bed frame of wood

and rope covered by a fern-stuffed mattress. A second steeper stairway led to a storage area under the eaves.

Josepha had readied the house, floors swept, a bucket of river water and a stack of firewood near the stove. "I'll send my husband soon with soup for your family tonight," she said. "For now, settle in. You and the children must be so tired. I am so happy to have you as my *auzotarrak*." Giving Arroxa another hug, she left.

Arroxa sat heavily in a chair to feed the crying baby. Antonio, happy to be free from the confines of the basket, ran through the rooms of the house, calling out to Lina. The two played hide and seek and climbed up and down the stairs. Pilar, peevish from her long day, clung to Arroxa's skirt, wanting to be held. Arroxa looked around at the disarray feeling suddenly overwhelmed with all there was to do. Sebriano unwrapped a box of matches, lit a lantern, then a fire in the hearth. He placed a pot of water to warm. Then, meeting Arroxa's eye, nodded and headed out the door in the direction of the *errota*.

She washed and swaddled the baby in clean sheep skins and placed him in a nest of blankets in a box to fall asleep. She sorted the bundles and boxes in search of food, dishes, and candles. She put Lina to work carrying bedding and pillows up the stairs, grateful for her desire to help and for her strong legs.

Sebriano returned from the mill carrying a pail of soup he handed to Arroxa, "From Josepha," he said. On his back hung a bundle of corn husks. "I found these in the *errota*, enough for a small bed for these two, they should sleep near us tonight." Sebriano dragged the bag up the stairs to the front bedroom, the children clambering behind begging to help.

"I can do it, *Aita*!" and, "Me too, me too!"

From upstairs came the sound of their voices and the shuffling of feet as Sebriano stuffed the corn husks into the bedding sacks.

Rain begin to fall as the family sat to eat the soup with cheese and cold *talua*. Arroxa tidied the room, and one-by-one washed the children's faces and hands to ready them for bed. Sebriano fed the *txakur* scraps, stacked more firewood inside, refilled the water bucket, secured the red window shutters and the door. They led the children upstairs by candle light. Lina and Antonio settled on a pallet on the floor, Pilar in a nest of blankets at the foot of the bed, Manuel in his box. They were asleep almost at once.

Exhausted, Arroxa and Sebriano changed and climbed into bed. They lay side by side in the unfamiliar darkness, the continuous tumble of the Nive just outside the window. Their thoughts drifted back over the day's events, absorbing all the newness. He took her hand. "It'll be good for us, Arroxa, you will see," he said. She turned on her side, lay her head on the pillow next to his and fell asleep.

During the night, steady rain pattered on the roof, dripped from small unseen holes down the walls and puddled on the floor of the room. Arroxa tossed feverishly, strange and senseless dreams floating through her sleep: her *Aita'*s face speaking wordlessly, the swaying rhythm of the mule, her children's arms reaching for her. Sebriano stirred next to her and she woke to wetness on her face and pillow.

"The roof is leaking," came his voice. They pulled themselves from beneath the blankets and, in the darkness, slid the bed and the pallet of sleeping children to a dryer corner of the room. Then they settled back into uneasy sleep.

Morning came, leaden and damp. Arroxa woke in the semi-light, the dreams an unsettling feeling just below the surface. Her head ached, her body felt heavy, weary, chilled. She dressed, gathered the mewing baby in her arms and moved quietly past her sleeping family down the stairs to the kitchen. She added wood to the still warm ashes, put water on to heat, and sat in a chair. She propped her leg on the stool and nursed Manuel.

Soon, Lina tiptoed down the stairs, tousled and sleepy-eyed. "*Ama*," she asked climbing on the chair next to Arroxa, "are we going home today?"

"Ah, *txikia*, we live here now," she sighed, putting her arm around Lina and drawing her in close. "This is our new home."

Sebriano, with Pilar in his arms, emerged from the stairway followed by Antonio. Laying the baby in his box, Arroxa made coffee and prepared *talua* and honey, then helped the children dress for the day, buttoning dresses and tying rope sandals. Sebriano stood eating his *talua* and sipping coffee, then went outside to see what could be done with the roof.

Arroxa begin the work of unpacking, sorting, storing, setting up household. The cool drizzle confined the children to the house, underfoot and irritable, too little to occupy them. When Sebriano returned to the house in late morning, dirty and wet from roof repairs, Arroxa sat, weary and feverish, amidst the disarray.

"You're not feeling well?" he asked Arroxa.

"*Bai*, my head aches and I feel so tired," she said. "I need to lie down for a time."

"I'll take Lina and Antonio to inspect the *errota*. It'll give you some time for rest and peace," he said.

Sebriano gathered the two older children, wrapped them in jackets and shawls, and they headed out the door. With effort, Arroxa climbed the stairs to the bedroom and settled the restive Pilar at the foot of her bed for a nap. She lay down, baby at her side, and closed her eyes.

* * * * * * * * *

Arroxa woke from her nap to the sound of the baby stirring beside her. The rain had stopped, and through the window, evening fell in shades of gray, casting shadows into the corners of the still empty room. Pilar was gone from her nest at the foot of the bed. She sat up slowly, feeling her head clear of sleepiness and fever. She lifted Manuel, pulling open her gown, and set his eager mouth to her breast.

Through the doorway, she could see yellow lantern light from the kitchen pooling at the top of the stairs. She smelled the fragrant musty wood smoke of the evening fire and heard the sounds of pots clanking and chairs rasping. Layered over, came her children's voices, a high, sweet cadence, harmonized with the deeper murmur of their *Aita*.

Arroxa leaned back and settled under the warm blanket. In her arms, Manuel murmured and suckled. Gently, she held his small waving fist between her fingers. She ached with the losses this journey had brought. But, in that moment, sitting peacefully in her new *etxe*, she felt inside, first a trickle, then a stream of what she knew to be hope. It filled her chest, raising her heart on its tide.

* * * * * * * * * *

Arroxa could not have known, in 1902, that this etxe would remain her family's home for almost a hundred years. Three generations of Bidegains grew up within its walls. The etxe and errota still stand today on the banks of the river Nive. The house was officially named Etxe Roxenia in her honor.

Her oldest children, including my Amatxi Lina, also traveled far from home, to America, looking for opportunity. They brought their Basque heritage and family stories with them.

Glossary of Basque
Words and Expressions

Aita – father

Aitatxi – grandfather (pronounced ai-ta-chee)

Amatxi – grandmother (ama-chee)

Ama – mother

ardiak – sheep (plural), *ardia* – sheep (singular) (ar-dee-ak)

ardoa – wine

auzotarrak – first or close neighbors who cooperate together in the Basque tradition (*auzotar(ra)*, singular)

bai – yes (as in the English 'buy')

baserri – Basque farm or farmhouse

errota – mill powered by river water for grinding grain

errotaria – miller

etxe(a) – house, *etxeak* – houses (e-che-a)

fronton – playing court with a high rock wall for playing *pilota*, often located in the village square

laka – measure of ground corn used to barter

makila – traditional Basque walking stick used by sheep herders to guide their flocks (ma-kee-la)

milesker – thank you (mil-eshker)

mus – card game originating in the Basque region (moos)

ongi etorri – welcome (ong-ee etor-ee)

pilota – a Basque ball game played against a wall or *fronton* on a court

talua – cakes made of ground corn and cooked on a grill (ta-loo-a)

txakoa – bag made of sheepskin used to transport wine (cha-koh-a)

txakur(ra) – dog (cha-kura)

txapela — beret (cha-pe-la)

txikia — little one, Basque term of
endearment (chee-kee-a)

txistu — Basque 3-holed flute or pipe
(chee-stoo)

zapi — headscarf worn by Basque women,
tied in knots at the back of the head (sap-
ee)

About the Author

Michelle Petitte grew up in southern California where she attended Basque picnics and listened to a lifetime of stories told by her Amatxi Lina. During a visit to the Pays Basque as a young girl, Michelle felt the pull of the culture and its people. Now she is writing Lina's stories, combining her memories, her mother's notes, interviews with family and friends, and research on Basque culture and history. The stories begin here, with Arroxa, Michelle's great grandmother.

The author, Michelle Petitte,
in the window of Etxe Roxenia, 1974

Made in the USA
Middletown, DE
18 March 2020